Our cover photograph is of
Montezuma Castle National Monument in Camp Verde, Arizona.

Above, hikers move towards the ruins of Montezuma Castle in the distance.

Over 600 years ago, the prehistoric Sinagua Indians occupied this five-story, 20 room limestone cliff dwelling. It stands today above Beaver Creek as one of the best preserved ruins in the nation. Mistakenly, early settlers in the region named the structure after the Aztec Emperor Montezuma assuming at the time that it was his ancient castle. In truth, the dwelling was abandoned nearly a century before the Emperor was even born. So, it was neither a castle nor occupied by Montezuma, yet it bares his name.

This view looking west over Cottonwood from Rocking Chair Road Reveals the Mingus Mountains in the background.

The lovely Verde Valley in Northern Arizona is a treasure trove of beauty, archeological wonders and enjoyable adventures for tourists and natives alike.

Beaver Creek just east of Sedona on Beaver Creek Road. This romantic creek also runs just below Montezuma Castle

The Verde River, a convenient watering spot for horses, is photographed from the bridge on Highway 89A.

Montezuma Well is not actually a well but a limestone sinkhole, a collapsed cavern filled with water, in McGuireville. Like a desert oasis, over a million gallons of water flow each day continuously providing sustenance to all creatures. It spans 368 feet across and is 55 feet deep. To this day, the Indians believe the water comes from the center of the earth and scientists remain mystified as to the actual physical source of the wellsprings. What is known, however, is that a high concentration of dissolved carbon dioxide measured at 600 times higher than most aquatic environments exhibits a consequential lack of oxygen. While a unique ecosystem with several plants and animals found nowhere else on earth flourish, other species such as fish cannot survive.

Tuzigoot Ruins in Clarkdale crowns this hilltop with an ancient pueblo spanning 42 acres. Tuzigoot, an intricate village or pueblo, was built by a culture known as the Sinagua. 110 rooms within the ruins include second and third story structures. The building began around A.D. 1000. The Sinagua were agriculturalists who traded with other tribes for hundreds of miles. The people left the area around 1400.

In the period around 1870, Fort Verde was the primary base for General Crook's U.S. Army scouts and soldiers who were dispatched to protect the settlers in the new territory. The officer's quarters as well as the Fort's museum are open to visitors exhibiting artifacts that display life on the frontier during that era.

These men were enlisted to represent the historic line of Cavalry during the taming of the West in Arizona's early heritage.

The Verde River meanders through Cottonwood.

The prolific prickly pear cactus (below) found in this terrain can be used for medicinal purposes. Everything from asthmatic conditions to earaches, minor rashes, sunburn, and even snakebites can be treated with this cactus split in half or as a poultice.

Pecks Lake

Another favorite spot for visitors and birdwatchers is the picturesque Pecks Lake. Here, wild ducks glide gracefully over the surface of the water in a golden moment. In the distance sits the old mining town of Jerome.

On the next pages, this section of Cottonwood originally built in the early 1900's, is known as Old Town. In the early days of prohibition, this street was famous for the best booze in Arizona and was frequented by notables from far and wide. It really got hot in 1917 when Arizona's Bootleg King, Big Joe Hall, caused a fire when his still blew up and burned down most of the neighborhood. It was rebuilt only to be destroyed yet again by Thomas Moore's prized still that blew up April 19th, 1925 at 3 a.m. taking along with it 14 homes in the blaze. On the night before the fire, George H. Brooks, a renowned minister, Doctor of Divinity & lecturer from Los Angeles who was holding seminars in the area, was staying at the Cottonwood Hotel. He predicted the town would see its biggest catastrophe ever. Not only was he right, but he was also the one fatality in the disaster. Some say he was murdered that night and has been seen walking the upper hallway of the old Cottonwood Hotel at the end of the street. The mystery of his death remains a secret perhaps still whispered in the ears of visitors to Old Town. Poised at the very end of the street is the tiny old jail built specifically for Joe the Bootlegger who spent 10 long months in a 5 x 6 cell, which is part of the Old Town Visitors Tour.

PHOTO BY KATHLEEN FRANCIS

A stormy day on Page Springs Road

Old Town still has the charm of the its wild history. Tuzigoot looms in the background reminding us of the roots of the ancient past of this valley.

LIQUOR
FINE FO
Verde Valley
HUMANE SOCIETY
PACKAGE
LIQUORS
APS

A closer look at **Tuzigoot National Monument.**
Years from now, what will remain of today's structures
that hug the base of the snow covered Mingus Mountains.

***Sycamore Canyon** rests in pristine beauty as you drive on the road leaving Clarkdale where the road to Tuzigoot National Monument begins.*

A horse ranch in Camp Verde

PHOTO BY KATHLEEN FRANCIS

PHOTO BY KATHLEEN FRANCIS

A pumpkin patch in Camp Verde on a moody autumn day

Founded in 1876, Jerome began as a tent town and grew into a booming mining community of 15,000 in the 20's. Known as the wickedest town in the West, this copper rich site half way up Cleopatra Hill in the Mingus Mountains delivered almost a billion dollars of copper to U.S. industry. Mining with explosives and unsafe conditions left many a fallen fortune seeker. Long hours and hard work for good pay created a different kind of opportunity for adventurous women who 'serviced' the miners after hours. Healthy bank accounts grew for some of these high-spirited 'ladies' as they claimed their place in history. World War I brought prosperity, growth and labor unrest. Billed as a three shift town, their 13 hotels, 21 bars and 8 houses of ill repute flourished until the great depression in the 30's when production slowed down.

World War II revived activity for a short time, but by 1953, after 70 years of blasting copper, the environment had a chance to begin to recover. The flower children of the 60's picked up property for a song and artists and crafts people planted the seed for a new birth of Jerome as an artist's haven for tourists to explore and bring home treasures. This 'ghost town', reinvented with as few as a hundred people, used its heritage to become the not-to-be-missed Arizona gem it is today.

Here in Jerome,
the **High House**
still stands as
one of the original
structures.

HIGH HOUSE
HIGH HOUSE SHOP

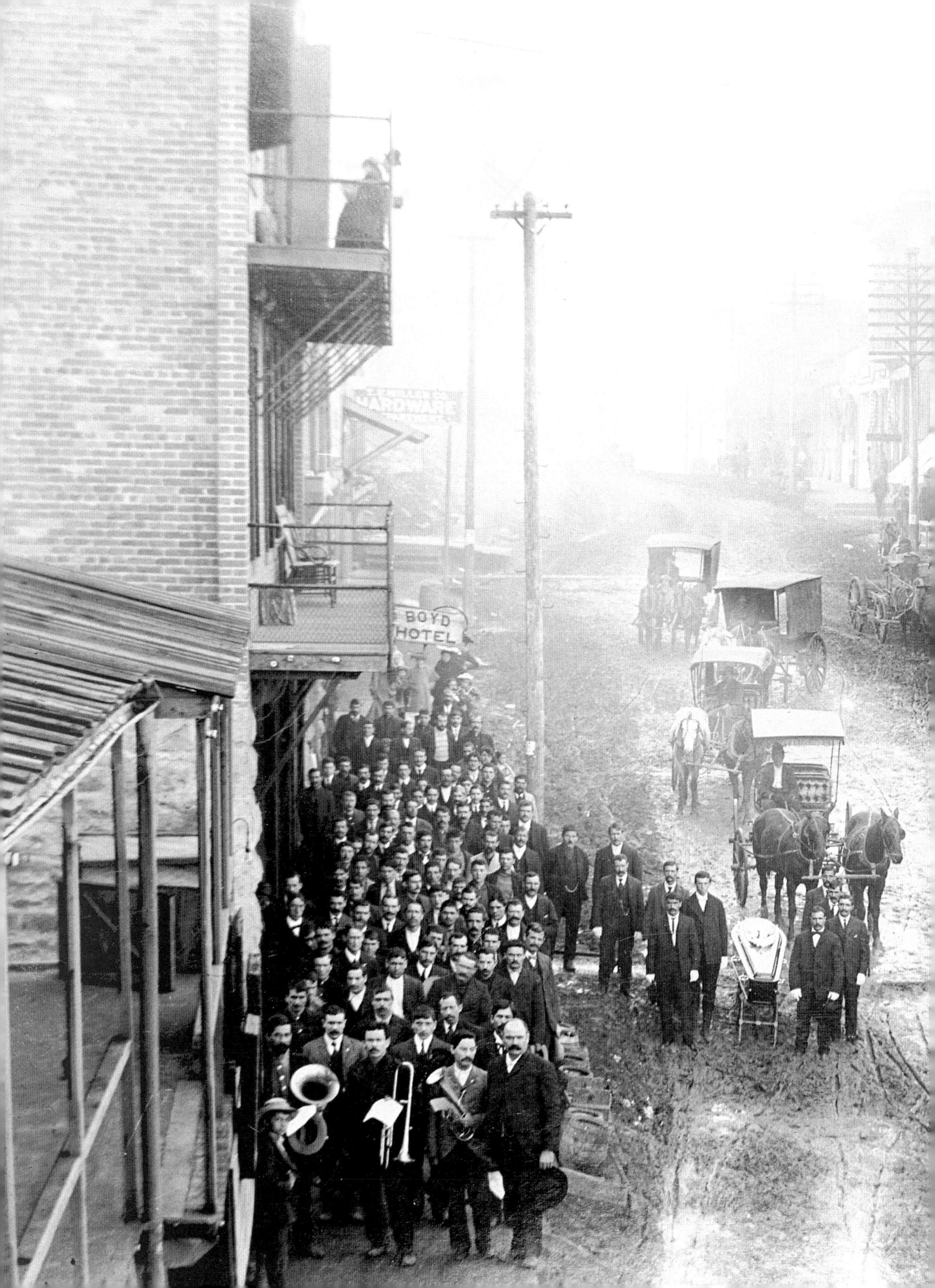
HARDWARE
BOYD
HOTEL

A rare photograph taken in the late 1800's gives a glimpse of life in that era. A misty funeral parade of perhaps a fallen miner was captured as his soul is set to rest. Down the road, Jerome's cemetery sits atop a hill overlooking the vast vista clear to the San Francisco peaks in distant Flagstaff.

This well-worn sign side by side with the old mining equipment retains the past in rust and iron. Note the famous 'J' resting at the highest peak of Jerome's landscape.

The shot below gives you a perspective of the old graveyard perched high on one of the hills in Jerome. These departed souls have an eternal view of the magnificent panorama of Cottonwood, Sedona and Flagstaff.

The fascinating wrought iron and cement grave coverings in this 1800's cemetery in Jerome was customary for the times...grave robbers were discouraged by such practices. Inscriptions on the stones provoke the imagination rendering questions about the lives of those whose bones rest on this hill. What stories might be told of this rugged land at a time when copper was carved out of the hill and futures were molded in the Wild West? If you look closely at the photograph above, you'll see a spirit captured just above the wrought iron fence towards the front of this old grave. *(Photos on these pages were taken by Kathleen Francis©.)*

The Gold King Mine is a graveyard for turn of the century trucks, tractors, construction and mining equipment. Truly an unprecedented outdoor museum not to be missed. To keep looters out, this grave marker spoof reads, "Here lies so cold & tense the last S.O.B. that climbed this fence!"

The road winds into Jerome where homes were built on the steep slopes of the rocky hills.

Some of the buildings in Jerome came tumbling down from the blasts that rocked the copper rich hills in the early 1900's.

The Jerome "Y" loops around and is peppered with curio shops and galleries of local artisans.

The House of Joy

Now a prestigious restaurant, this once was a house of ill repute for the miners who toiled by day bringing copper from the rich Cleopatra Hill in Jerome.

The Powder Box Church and Douglas Mansion

James "Rawhide Jimmy" Douglas, once owner of the Little Daisy Mine, built this stately mansion in 1916 for his family. Often used to house and entertain visiting mining officials and investors in its "heyday," the historic adobe-brick structure now displays mining remnants of the past and is now the Jerome Historic State Park.

Nearby in the foreground is the Powder Box Church, which got its name because Sabino Gonzalez built it with the wood from dynamite crates used to blast copper from the Cleopatra Mine.

Jerome covets their old buildings and ageless charm. These vines, grown against the brick for years untold, turn crimson red each year. The Holy Family Church across the street is frequented by thousands of visitors sending up their prayers from this elevated spot in old Jerome.

Downtown Jerome is still quaint - the famous Spirit House, a local saloon in the center of downtown, still stages live music with local musicians that play long into the night.

In the foreground rests Tuzigoot Monument with Jerome nestled at the foothills of the snow covered Mingus Mountains.

The peaceful Verde River

A shallow pond in Cornville is an oasis for these horses. This photo, along with several others in this book, appeared in Arizona Highways magazine.

This picturesque 1975 shot of a lazy day in the lives of three lucky Arizona kids cruisin' down famous Oak Creek near Cornville captures the imagination.

Cottonwood from the westside with
Sedona in the far distance.

This historical photo of Montezuma Castle was taken in 1923.

THE ANCIENT REMNANTS OF A SINAGUAN INDIAN VILLAGE

According to historians, the first permanent settlers in the Verde Valley were the Hohokam (Pima for "those who have gone"). They were farming people who settled here shortly after A.D. 600. They cultivated corn, beans, squash and cotton and watered them by irrigation. The Sinagua (Spanish for "without water") inhabited the nearby foothills and the plateau beyond the valley in about 1125. The Sinagua were pithouse dwellers and dry farmers depending on rain for their crops. Around 1150, the Sinagua began building their large pueblos, often on hilltops or in cliffs. The villages at Montezuma and Tuzigoot reached their present size in the 1300's and were occupied for another century. In the early 1400's, the Sinagua abandoned the entire valley. No one can say why - perhaps too much pressure on the land, perhaps conflict with the Yavapai, disease or draught. Whatever the reason, survivors were probably absorbed into villages in the north.

Sometimes referred to as the Anasazi, the Sinagua were peaceful village dwellers. They lived principally by farming and supplemented their staple crops by hunting and gathering. Because of the abundant water in the central valley, crops did well and wild game stayed close to the water supply. Deer, antelope, elk, rabbit, bear, muskrat, turtle and duck were staples in a diet that leaned heavily on corn. The Indians here were comparatively well off in the important commodity of salt. A few miles from the present town of Camp Verde, evidence of salt mining by the Sinagua was discovered.

The Sinagua were considered fine artisans. Stone tools such as axes, knives, hammers, manos and metates for grinding corn are found in the museums. Using bone weaving tools, they fashioned garments of cotton. Ornaments were made from shells, turquoise and a local red stone for adornment.

Obviously demonstrating their innovative building skills, the tribes over time improved their structures. Some of the early more fragile dwellings may have been due to the quality of the local rock. It was fairly soft and split unevenly. Walls at Tuzigoot are massive but poorly balanced. Yet Montezuma Castle, which admittedly is well protected, was so securely built that it has stood for over 600 years and is considered one of the most well-preserved prehistoric structures in the Southwest.

Clear Creek
runs through the old Bull Pen Ranch, which is now part of Forest Service land and is designated as recreational territory for visitors from around the world.

Old Barn at the Bull Pen Ranch - this site burned down in the 50's.

Oak Creek Valley

The excursion train runs along the Verde River between Clarkdale and Perkinsville. Their tour includes the Sinagua Indian Ruins, a pass through the 680 ft. man-made tunnel, and the only passageway along the North Verde River with a chance to observe the protected wilderness preservation and its abundant wildlife.

The Road to Perkinsville

The train passes over the bridge on its route to Perkinsville.

This Perkinsville corral is made with hand-cut tree posts 'old west' style.

Old houses in Perkinsville

A rare
pack rat nest

These are the gravestones of Stanley and Betty Perkins for which the town was named. The sentiment on Stanley's tombstone, "This is my church, this beautiful land" says it all.

About Bob Bradshaw, your photographic tour guide...

Perhaps nothing captures the truth like a photograph. Words inevitably carry one's opinions. A photograph is simply that unaltered moment in time, constant and forever for the sensitive to perceive. This has been Bob Bradshaw's contribution as he began recording on celluloid what was often a countryside yet untouched by the developer's blueprint on our land. With this book, part of our nation's history lives on. Since 1950, Bob has been a major contributor to Arizona Highways Magazine. He has been a rancher most of his life and was involved in nearly every motion picture made in the region. Well into his eighties at the time of this publication, he continues to enthusiastically snap his way through our planet's scenic beauty. He has witnessed what once was and holds a position, along with his lineage, to preserve as much of our pristine landscape as is humanly possible. With this, he hopes to inspire your support to do the same...at any opportunity, wherever you may live, to respect and protect what no "man" can create or replace.

Bob's lineage bred much of who he is. His father, John Bradshaw, a champion athletic coach, trained the world record-breaking runner, Jesse Owens. Bob's uncle, Marion, a university professor, was a published writer and photographer traveling the world in an era when that was no small feat. Bob's sons continue the traditions of this heritage. His awareness of the delicate balance between man's needs and the disappearance of our pristine landscape is always present in his mind. Together, he hopes that the solutions will be met with sensitivity to the precious land that he so loves.

This photo of Bob Bradshaw was captured by Kathleen Francis

Cliff Castle Casino is run by the Yavapai Apache Nation and is frequented by locals and tourists alike looking to bring home a treasure of another kind.

Don Robertson (above) along with his artist wife, Terry, operate the historic Gold King Mine designed to transport you back into Jerome's unique past.

Kokopelli, playing his flute, is known as the trickster in Arizona mythology. Perhaps the biggest in the land is in front of the Montezuma Castle Trading Post near Camp Verde off Hwy 17.

Some of the long-standing businesses that service the tourist community include the Best Western Cottonwood Inn where warm hospitality abounds.

The Mining Museum is an excellent resource for visitors to explore old Jerome's colorful past.